Time to go Home

by **David Orme**
Illustrated by **Alek Sotirovski**

FULL FLIGHT

Titles in the Full Flight Thrills and Spills series:

The Knight Olympics	Jonny Zucker
Pied Piper of London	Danny Pearson
The Science Project	Jane A C West
Gorilla Thriller	Richard Taylor
Clone Zone	Jillian Powell
Clowning Around	Helen Orme
Time to go Home	David Orme
Haunted Car	Roger Hurn
Dinosaur Rampage	Craig Allen
Rubbish Ghost	Jillian Powell

Badger Publishing Limited
Suite G08, Stevenage,
Hertfordshire SG1 2DX
Telephone: 01438 791 037
Fax: 01438 791 036
www.badgerlearning.co.uk

Time to go Home ISBN 978-1-84926-995-7

Text © David Orme 2013
Complete work © Badger Publishing Limited 2013

All rights reserved. No part of this publication may be reproduced, stored in any form or by any means mechanical, electronic, recording or otherwise without the prior permission of the publisher.

The right of David Orme to be identified as author of this Work has been asserted by him in accordance with the Copyright, Designs and Patents Act 1988.

Publisher: Susan Ross
Senior Editor: Danny Pearson
Designer: Fiona Grant
Illustrator: Alek Sotirovski

Time to go Home

Contents

Chapter 1	Boring!	5
Chapter 2	Over the Fence	11
Chapter 3	Bones!	16
Chapter 4	Putting it Right	20
Chapter 5	The Experiment	25

Sundials   30

Questions about the Story   32

New words:

sundial   interested

scientist   experiment

disgusting   skeletons

Main characters:

Jade

James

Chapter 1

Boring!

James and Jade's mum stood in front of the TV. "We're going to stay with Uncle Ken next week," she said.

"Oh no! Do we have to? It's boring at his place!" sighed James.

"We can't even take our laptops.
He doesn't have the internet!"
snapped Jade.

James and Jade hated going to Uncle Ken's house. There was nothing to do there. It was right out in the country. All he ever talked about was his garden.

They hated gardening!

"Take plenty of books to read,"
said Mum.

They liked reading. But they didn't want to do that for the whole week.

"You can go for walks," she carried on saying.

"That's boring too," sighed Jade.

Mum and Dad started to get cross.

James and Jade thought that they had better shut up. There wasn't any choice. They would have to go.

The first day was really bad. Uncle Ken wanted to show them all the work he had done in his garden.

He went on and on about it. "Look at these! Isn't it exciting? I've never grown red ones before!"

James and Jade tried to look interested, but it wasn't easy.

At the bottom of the garden was a fence. Big, leafy branches hung over it.

"What's over there, Uncle Ken?" asked Jade.

Uncle Ken looked cross.

"A mess, that's what! There's an empty house over there. The garden hasn't been looked after for years! All those seeds blow over into my garden!"

Jade thought that the garden over the fence was much more interesting than Uncle Ken's. But she didn't say so.

Chapter 2

Over the Fence

James and Jade just had to get away from Uncle Ken and his garden. They decided to go out for a walk, even if it was boring.

"Where shall we go?" asked James.

Jade answered, "I want to have a look at that garden."

"Not Uncle Ken's garden again! We've been round it dozens of times!"

"No, the other garden. The weedy one over the fence," Jade said with a smile.

Uncle Ken had told them more about it yesterday evening.

A scientist called John Kent had lived in the house. When his wife died he stopped looking after the garden.

Uncle Ken said that he still owned the house, but he hadn't been seen there for ages.

"What do you want to go there for?" asked James.

"I just do. It could be interesting. That Kent man might have murdered his wife and buried her in the garden!"

James looked at her, "You've been reading too many stories!"

They decided they would go and take a look. Anything was better than hanging around at Uncle Ken's.

The front of the house was a real mess. Weeds grew everywhere. The windows were broken.

"Let's go and see the garden," said Jade.

"Jade, you can't just go into someone's garden!" James looked worried.

"What's the matter? Scared? Come on, just a quick look!"

James looked up and down the road. There was no one to see them. The front gate was difficult to open. They pushed hard and it opened at last. A weedy path went round the side of the house.

They were in – but what would they find there?

Chapter 3

Bones!

The garden was very quiet. There were no birds. That was strange – Uncle Ken's garden was full of them. Even the trees looked old and sad here.

One tree had apples growing on it. James tried to eat one. He spat it out.

"It tastes disgusting!" he said.

A narrow path went through the bushes. It was very twisty.

Soon they couldn't see the gate. At the end of the path they found an open space. In the middle of it was a sundial.

"Look!" said James in horror. "Bones!"

On the ground by the sundial were two skeletons. One of them was still wearing ragged clothes.

"Perhaps he did murder his wife!" said Jade. "Quick, let's get out of here! He may still be around, hiding in the house!"

They ran back along the path. It seemed a long way to the gate.

"What's that up ahead?" said James.

It was the sundial! They had come back to the middle of the garden!

They couldn't work out what had happened. There was only one path. How could they have gone wrong?

They set off again along the twisty path.

A few minutes later, they were back at the sundial. Now they started to get really frightened.

James had an idea. He decided to go off the path and push through the bushes.

It was too hard. The bushes all had thorns on them. Soon he was covered with scratches. He decided to give up. He pushed his way back to the path.

How were they going to get back?

Chapter 4

Putting it Right

Jade saw something else under the bushes. More bones! They were bones of birds and animals this time.

Jade and James tried not to panic.

They decided to try the path again. Soon they were back at the sundial.

There was something very strange about this garden. People and animals could get in. But once they were in they couldn't get out again.

Then they starved to death!

Jade and James tried shouting, but the thick trees and bushes blocked their voices.

They sat down by the sundial. It had been a cloudy morning but now the sun was coming out. Most of the garden was shady. Only the sundial was in sunshine.

Jade was trying to think how to escape from the garden. She was older than her brother. She was in charge.

James looked at the sundial. He knew how they worked. There was one on the wall of his school.

A part of the sundial was always in shadow from the sun. The shadow showed you what time it was.

"This sundial is all wrong!" said James.

The times were marked on a metal plate. James found he could turn it. He checked his watch.

"What are you doing?" asked Jade.

"I'm putting the sundial right."

"Don't waste your time on that! Help me think of a way to get out of here!"

But James had already turned the sundial to the right time.

Suddenly, in the garden around them, birds flew down and started to sing.

James and Jade looked at each other in surprise.

Chapter 5

The Experiment

"It was a test!" said James. "You can't get out of here until the sundial is right. Those skeletons must be from people who couldn't work it out."

"Right," said Jade. "Stop talking and let's get out of here!"

They ran down the path. James grabbed another apple from the apple tree as he ran past.

It was juicy and sweet.

They ran round the last corner, past the house, and there was the front gate.

They pushed their way through and banged it shut behind them. They kept running as fast as they could. Soon they were back at their uncle's house.

"That was really scary!" said James.

Jade was thinking about what had happened to them. "That man Uncle Ken told us about, John Kent. He was a scientist. Maybe he was working on an experiment with the sundial that went wrong," she said.

"Could be. But where is he now? Surely he wouldn't just walk away and leave it," James wondered.

Jade had an awful thought.

"Maybe he was one of the skeletons. Or maybe... he's still in the house. He might have got trapped in there and been unable to get out to change the sundial."

They went out into Uncle Ken's garden. Over the fence, the birds had stopped singing.

They had tried to fly away, but they couldn't leave the garden.

In the middle of the garden, a ray of sunlight had lit up the sundial.

Once again, it was telling the wrong time.

Sundials

How does a sundial work?

A sundial has a pointer in the middle of it called a gnomon (sounds like 'no-mon'). The gnomon casts a shadow when the sun shines. The shadow moves as the sun moves across the sky. The place where the shadow falls is marked with the hours of the day.

That sounds easy!

Well, it is more complicated than that. In the summer, the sun is high in the sky. In the winter, it is low down. This can affect where the shadow falls on the sundial. Where you live in the world is also important.

This makes it quite difficult to make an accurate sundial.

In the past, people would get up when the sun came up, have a midday meal when the sun was overhead (noon), then go to bed when it got dark. But some people did need to know the time. The first sundials we know about were made by the Egyptians over 5500 years ago.

Be a human sundial!

Face the sun on a sunny day. Get someone to measure how long your shadow is, and write it down. Do this again every hour in the same spot, checking the time on your watch. The next day you will be able to work out what time it is by looking at the length of your shadow!

Remember, though, as the seasons change, your shadow will get longer and shorter, (and you will grow taller!)

Questions about the Story

Why did Jade think the messy garden next door was more interesting than Uncle Ken's garden?

It was wrong for James and Jade to go into someone's garden without permission. What would you have done? Why?

Who do you think the human bones might have belonged to? What do you think happened to Mr Kent?

Why is it important to know exactly what the time is?

How many reasons can you think of why a watch is better than a sundial?